To John
In poetic friendship
Richard 27/3/18

CW01633215

R[illegible]t

There they live much longer

Indigo Dreams Publishing

First Edition: There they live much longer
First published in Great Britain in 2018 by:
Indigo Dreams Publishing
24, Forest Houses
Cookworthy Moor
Halwill
Beaworthy
Devon
EX21 5UU

www.indigodreams.co.uk

Richard Westcott has asserted his right under the Copyright, Designs and Patents Act 1988 to be identified as the author of this work.
© 2018 Richard Westcott

ISBN 978-1-910834-78-7

British Library Cataloguing in Publication Data. A CIP record for this book can be obtained from the British Library.

This book is sold subject to the condition that it shall not, by way of trade or otherwise, be lent, re-sold, hired out, or otherwise circulated without the author's and publisher's prior consent in any form of binding or cover other than that in which it is published and without a similar condition including this condition being imposed on the subsequent purchaser.

Designed and typeset in Palatino Linotype by Indigo Dreams.
Cover design: Detail from woodcut '*Picasso and the orchid*' by Judith Westcott www.judithwestcott.co.uk
Author photo by Chris Chapman
Printed and bound in Great Britain by 4edge Ltd.
Papers used by Indigo Dreams are recyclable products made from wood grown in sustainable forests following the guidance of the Forest Stewardship Council.

To Sarah – my love and thanks

There they live much longer
is Richard's debut collection of poetry.

CONTENTS

A Wise Man Takes His Leave

I can already see the earth
in all its fine reality –
a sphere of lovely colours,
the mountains smooth where precious stones
are uncorroded – every sense
is clearer. There they live much longer.

Mighty streams descend and mingle.
Dear friends it is determined –
Echecrates, Simmias, Cebes –
your time will come as mine has now.
It's nearly sunset. Bring in my cup.

I shall ask for a gentle voyage.
The earth awaits. I walk its surface
for a moment I wait too
for descent and rearrangement.

Let me lie down now.
Farewell to you and to myself –
the icy tide is rising

from feet to legs to waist.
Observe the customs. There they live

much longer.

Corporal Yukio Araki, age 17
of the 72nd Shinbu Squadron, 27th May 1945

The school girls wave their cherry blossom branches
then he flies south towards Mount Kaimon,
wearing the Rising Sun, his waist hemmed in
by a thousand single stitches.

Yukio remembers the flop-eared puppy
passed between them the night before –
his life ahead – and those branches that waved
between girls, releasing their fragrance.

There is the spirit: there in the passage and passing
from one to another – each girl with her branch,
and of one little dog who is scented by milk
with no fears of his own, yet

shifting his weight to balance himself.
Yukio flies on. He must aim for the middle –
the gap between gunwale and waterline –
while bearing the Rising Sun.

Each stitch disappears before it emerges.
The school girls have gone back indoors.
Some other pilot will steady the bowl
which whitens the tips of a puppy dog's ears.

Yukio has said goodbye to the mountain.
The gap narrows. As he draws close
He's sure he sees waving again, and deep
in his throat as he cries, he tastes milk.

(Kamikaze pilots wore a headband with the Rising Sun, a belt of a thousand stitches (one each from a different woman, it was said) and flew past the southernmost tip of Japan, Mount Kaimon, on their final mission.)

A Letter

Cara
ti saluto

you will not be surprised to hear
I have been depressed again.
I must tell you, my dear friend,
there is so much yet to know
of physics and organic chemistry
and phenomena that control
the making of a mayonnaise
or a simple vinaigrette.

Meanwhile here I sit at home
under the sketch of a barbed wire fence
and a Garibaldi poster
along with our two mothers.
Mine who's senile is ninety-one,
hers is blind and ninety-five –
totally blind for fifteen years.
I know that you will understand
my place is here. I cannot leave.

I have always tried. I can only write.
If I'm not for myself, who will be for me?
If not this way, how? If not now, then when?

Please excuse my themes' diversity –
the world is beautiful in all its variety.

It is time to end my letter.
My injured foot is slow to heal,
depression makes it hard to write.
I worry about my loss of memory.
I have more doubts than convictions.

There is little left to say.
How many things we've seen and done
together. Thank you, you're very kind.

The indifferent rivers will keep flowing
and glaciers continue to grate.
Perhaps my books will live.
Tu sei gentile.

De profundis
Primo

This is a Man ...

There is no doubt, for –

amongst the blood, exploded organs,
juices – which until a moment ago
were separate in their places –
now mixed up as in children's play,
thrown jelly stuck with fragments
which should have been retained,
smashed glasses where presumably
there was once a face,
arms flung out in an embrace,
a still shod foot, gardener's nails –

one sleeve has ridden up
a scrawny forearm to reveal
those small blue numbers
174517.

No, there is no doubt,
This is a Man. No bomb was dropped,
just a willing step into a welcoming stairwell –
far from firearms, whips and violence,
communal showers and Zyklon B –
with mother upstairs and wife gone out.
At home.
At last.

No doubt.

Another Letter

Once more I'm hearing voices.
I am cursed by words, those very words
which made me what I am and which
I draw on every day. And so I write...

more words, to try to say what I am feeling
and what it is I have to do. I feel certain
I am going mad again, with all these words.
I loved your letter, those words of yours.

Please use more to tell him, now I cannot
speak myself, he has been in every way
so very good ... words fail me in my time
of greatest need, with such a choice.

All started with the word, and this is where
it ends, in these words I write to you.
We are no more than words
spoken by someone else.

Now I must go to drown my voices –
both those within and those without –
in the sound of running waters
so dumb silence must resume.

Return

How long has passed? Birthdays come and go –
many happy returns – along with many another
death day. Along these meadows here
I walk where once you walked
to exchange harsh air for gentle water
still current carried to a distant bridge.

The children watched, later found you
here. The workman in the ditch
saw you pass, not to come back.
No return, although the birthdays
come and go and I return
in my present now to your passing past.

Bobby Sands' Final Sonnet 1st May 1981

There comes a time when hunger feeds upon
itself – when all that's left to eat is pain,
that hungry, angry pain which now has gone
to leave me almost satisfied again.
I had no appetite for this – but they
once punished me with diet No. 1 –
just bread and water each third day so they
gave me the taste of what might yet be done.
I lie upon a water bed and float
from football – left back – down the stream of time,
past siblings, Geraldine, that narrow vote,
through poetry and politics – and crime,
which now seems distant, like the hunger I
consumed in anger so that I could die.

Seneca in his bath

I am emperor of myself.

I have taught and sought
the truth within me.

Self correction must now be found
in the warmth that is around.
It is an old familiar warmth

I feel as never felt before.
The weight is eased, limbs arise
as if this body tries to float
away from friends and all that's here.

My heat is seeping out in clouds
which spread like smoke from unseen fires.
I have tried to make the most
of what I had and could achieve.
Happiness is won through strength

unequally distributed –
the strength I mean, for I love all
that's good and fine and rich
in both the world and in man's mind.
I have praised indifference
to all kinds of material goods

and have urged that each of us
must strive to find his virtue.
And it is so. I live as one who knows
the way to live and now to die.
It is not how one lives

but how one ought to live
and when the time arrives
how one ought to die.
The wreaths roll out in curlicues

unravelling lines of thread of red
which spread. Thus I extend.
This is my choice. And as I drift

my wish is his, and is fulfilled.
And thoughts are stretched like evening clouds

welcoming home the cooling sun.

Vice-Admiral Robert FitzRoy RN
in his dressing room, 30th April 1865

Every morning I pick up this razor
to set myself up to face the world.
Once again here I sit. Before myself
familiar things and my own face,
awaiting that which will be done.

The turning steel returns the light
flashing for a moment. I watch
and wait as it revolves – my face and eyes
but now the ceiling. Stars and planets
circle on, each fastened in its orbit.

Between my hands I hold the power
to rotate the firmament. I can make
all things spin and am omnipotent.
I am he who learnt to tell
what was to be before it happened

through the act of observation.
I can forecast. It has stopped.
Along a line all is contained,
everything comes to a point
within this leading edge

of no reflection. The tide has turned,
deep waters shift below me.
As the moon refills I am represented –
myself again within a widening stretch,
passing through predictable phases.

I took care to leave her sleeping,
dreaming as she would of what may be
assured. Where substance tapers down
to nothing, no pressure is required –
like a bow in a southern sea

the blade draws near. This time
there is no need to calculate speed –
time, travel and trajectory –
all will collide when I decide
to take command once more

for I have observed too long.
The signal has been given – with a flash.
Both hands obey and in a single stroke,
the predicted occurs. I touch land
and the great flood pours.

Lucretia's Last Words

You do not know what will take place
you who are mine in truth
you do not know. Not yet.
Hear me. Hear my voice

before I leave and give me
give me your word. I beg
you father and beloved husband
attend and act as I will now

so that conquest be avenged
both mine and yours. So brief
brief is beauty. Death leads
to overthrow. He is all.

And after it has taken place
I will not know nor ever hear
those future voices as they sing
these words that once were mine.

Companionship

I went to meet him, heaviness about me
weighing me down. I remember
that weight.

And his persuasion – take the story
now make it different, make it into
poetry.

The weight remained – I was reminded
while we walked, as I could feel
the pull

of hard wood, iron and steel bound up
in previous resolution, awaiting
my decision.

He never knew what I was carrying
on that occasion, of what had been
determined

and I was not to know this first time
how far we two would walk
together

nor the power that poetry holds
for those who write it – no, not yet, writer
as I was.

Ahead of us lay many choices,
ways to follow, which road to take,
and now

I knew that we had more to say
the weight felt less, I had decided
not this time,

not this time, at this first meeting.
We would have more. I put that
weight aside,

took up his friendship, lightening me
while we walked together, until
I had to leave.

(It is said that at his first and momentous meeting with Robert Frost, Edward Thomas was carrying a loaded revolver in his pocket.)

Lar Familiaris

Across this threshold I have passed
many times between my open hands
an offering, to sustain.

Now I approach the familiar step
once more, hands closed.
No collection dish today –

instead a pillow
like a cushion on the altar
awaits, with comfort.

Through inspiration I shall pass
across this threshold one last time –
my hands will open, to receive
the sustenance I pray for.

(Sylvia Plath laid her head in her unlit gas oven.)

E.H. and his Gun

This is how real men do it.
Here is my game gun
with which I shoot birds.
A father understands.
And a man like me needs
not one but two barrels.
My W. & C Scott & Son
has travelled far with me
and we go on together.

I have written enough.
There were always too many
far too many words.
A gun has not got much
to say but what is said
is to the point. I am
a man of iron who lives
and dies according to
his own determination.

Reflection

Suddenly glimpsed
who can this beauty be?
He stared and he stared
as his eyes opened wider
the moment prolonged
as his eyes opened wider
he stared and he stared
who can this beauty be?
Suddenly glimpsed

Love sprang like a fountain
he tried to draw nearer
but could not approach
the moment prolonged
present slipped past
the moment prolonged
but could not approach.
He tried to draw nearer
love sprang like a fountain.

Her words rang back again
calling his name
but she was no longer.
Gradually pining
he became rooted
gradually pining
but she was no longer
calling his name
her words rang back again

Unheard by a flower.
The water runs still
voices have faded
youth's wasted away
though beauty remains.
Youth's wasted away
voices have faded
the water runs still
unheard by a flower.

Eclipse

Birds fall silent at this false dusk.
As circles approach the edges of worlds
collide in a blur of first darkness.
An unusual coolness falls upon us.

You do not need to know the pain
when they were both put out. There is
no darkness to approach that black
when light is lost forever.

Worlds travel on to overlap.
At the centre an oval that grows
a widening eye still out of sight.
Nothing so dark as the pupil itself.

You do not need to see the pillars
as bodies move apart. I seized them
in a vision of destruction
and in bowing avenged the loss.

The light returns along with warmth.
From ends new starts are made.
Upon the pile of broken stones
a black bird starts to sing.

Upon a Threshold

I am standing here for now
warm and heavy in my secret
unaccustomed corset.
I am tightly laced in the embrace
of this death belt that will buoy me up
through smoky waters – I shall rise
dispersed and scattered
like a flock of little birds which fling
themselves in all directions
at the firing of a gun. Exploded
I will fly to meet a new found unity
in my disintegration into light
and flames with such a shaking.
I shall then become the many
past the tremor, recreated
for a better life beyond this death.
I am hugged and hold for now
my secret close against my heart
with feeding sparrows round my feet.

The Metamorphosis of Antinous

Here Osiris perished, to return
as god. Sweet ancient waters
now take me too, poised upon this brink.
It is so small a step from boy to man
to god. Now I brim with love
ready to die to give new life –
for you will flood, his tears will well
and temples spring their sacred fountains.
Great surge, pray take this body,
all I have, and carry me far from here
to long ago. Across this threshold
leaving flesh behind, I step to live
and to be loved afresh, in carved stone.

(Antinous, favourite (lover) of the Emperor Hadrian, drowned in the Nile, at the time of the festival of Osiris, god of death, life and fertility. A devastated Hadrian deified him, establishing his worship across the Empire, with thousands of statues to commemorate the new god.)

Hillside

He remembered the hill just outside town
where a barrier lines the tight bend.
He swung his legs over.

He did not know climbing the gate
quite how far to go. As
he slipped down the slope

he could not see through sycamore leaves
which one to choose.
He came to a stop.

He looked at his feet played on by shadows
passing like clouds. For now
he stood firm on the ground.

He slipped off his rucksack. Nobody noticed
it fall to the ground.
He took out the rope.

He tied it with care round the trunk of a tree
throwing the coil up over a branch.
He picked up the rest.

He climbed up the hill. The length was correct
to tie like a tie tucked under his collar.
He knotted the rope.

He adjusted the fit then patted his hair
as if in a mirror before leaving home.
He took in a breath.

He was ready to jump like a dive in the pool
unsure of the temperature no worse than that.
He went.

He did not hear the buzzard that cried
at little events played out on the ground
he was not to see. Now

he swung side to side, a heavy cloud shadow
picked up then lost by the trees.
He'd forgotten the hill.

Cleanthes

Draw near my friend – you must hear what I say.

Be of good cheer. I am old – soon to depart.
All that was made is created again.
Green grapes grow into clusters of ripeness,
afterwards raisins.

I have worked, I've worked hard
for wisdom and knowledge come hard to a striver
like me. Once I was strong and knew how to fight
but now I am ready to stop, to welcome the rest.
I haven't been eating.

The soreness improved
after fasting – they told me to eat again
but as I have travelled most of this road
I won't retrace steps.

He has his wish,
whose wish is to have enough: I desire nothing,
only to have what is meant to be.
There is no need for me to make changes, so
I will stay fasting.

Each step is a change,
not into what is not, but that which is yet to be.
Dear brother, give me your smile. Farewell
to this life. My fire will find new fuel.
Don't be distressed.

Your pain is yours
you make yourself, so you hold the power
to extinguish it. I have no pain. Now
you have heard the voice of one
who for a moment lived.

In the Office of Leipzig's Deputy Mayor, April 18th 1945

Cooling in her great coat
Regina Lisso lies for ever
sprawled across the corner
of the leather buttoned sofa.

She no longer sees her father
face down on his desk.
Nor her mother, pointing at the floor,
for her eyes are closed.

Frozen now in monochrome
she seems to sleep, her lips apart,
finger tips at rest.
The soldier stood and gazed

while spring sunshine fell
over her lovely throat.
He thought – the party's over
and leant to kiss her hand.

Her parents would not mind,
not now. All this happened
in a camera click, a capsule's
crunch. It smelt carbolic

that nurse's hand which fell
back into her lap. He straightened
her Red Cross arm band
and stood to attention

in the silence of suicide
which has nothing to say
Regina survives in her black and white photograph.
The soldier departed, unseen.

A Young Man's Questions

Is it self destructive to make an escape
an escape from a labyrinth and tyrant?

Is it self destructive to help craft a work
help craft a work never crafted before?

Is it self destructive to be carried away
carried away by that wonderful uplift?

Is it self destructive to turn into an angel
an angel to shepherds and ploughmen?

Is it self destructive to be mistaken
mistaken for a freshly-fledged god?

Is it self destructive to fly higher
higher than your father?

Is it self destructive to ask all these questions
these questions that cannot be answered?

Is it self destructive to have found immortality
immortality without answering the questions?

The Joy of Flotsam

To float free and be subject
to elements alone

to forego all self will
and abandon assumptions

to forget roles and to drift
from the tyranny of function

to begin in time to lose even identity

to have no need to find or be found...

Indigo Dreams Publishing Ltd
24, Forest Houses
Cookworthy Moor
Halwill
Beaworthy
Devon
EX21 5UU
www.indigodreams.co.uk